"Difficult as it is to accept that these are Claire's last words to her readers, they give to us, again, her unique voice and poetic vision. The thread of family binds these poems, as she writes about her daughter, 'It's then I see my father in her face, her *TaTa—grandfather* in her feet, just as I'd seen my mother in my niece.' Through a range of cultures and traditions ancestors come back to assert themselves—taxonomies of color in a series written in the voice of Frida Kahlo, the trickster figure Vishnu hiding behind a Lotus leaf, and the lyrics of Gulzar, an Urdu poet.

There are heartbreaking poems of elegy written for the children in 'After the Earthquake and Tsunami, 2011' and loss is leavened by the idea of return. She soothes her daughter, Vidya, 'miracle of my life' as she explains her grandfather has 'returned to Kerala where two river banks meet' and offers the couplet 'O my Daughter, you remind me our parents are still with us —'

As always, within Claire's work, there is the presence of a cat, Happy Joe, peering out from a window ledge, and communion with the natural world. There is the Satsuma orange tree in Tucson her parents won't see, yet a recognition that their souls or spirits might say, '*We're in Heaven — it's this beautiful garden.*' 'When we are gone, don't cry,' she tells her daughter, 'Like Vishnu, we are always with you.' These beautiful, intense poems return Claire to her readers, still grateful to hear her voice."

—ELLINE LIPKIN, AUTHOR OF *GIRLS' STUDIES*

Vidya's Tree

ヴィディヤの木

विद्या का पेड़

Vidya's Tree

ヴィディヤの木

विद्या का पेड़

a mother's legacy

CLAIRE KAGEYAMA-RAMAKRISHNAN

with an afterword by Rita Dove

BULL★CITY
PRESS

DURHAM, NORTH CAROLINA

Vidya's Tree

"Deep Sea Magic," "The Journey," "When My Daughter Wakes, I Tell Her,"
"For My Daughter," and "Vidya's Tree" first appeared in *Houston's Favorite
Poems*, edited by Robin Davidson.

Published in the United States of America

Library of Congress Cataloging-in-Publication Data

Kageyama-Ramakrishnan, Claire
Vidya's Tree: poems / by Claire Kageyama-Ramakrishnan
p. cm.
ISBN-13: 978-1-4951-7883-2

Book design by Spock and Associates
Cover art and author photograph by Rajesh Ramakrishnan

Published by
BULL CITY PRESS
1217 Odyssey Drive
Durham, NC 27713

www.BullCityPress.com

"I love you as deep as the sea."

David Van Buren and Tim Warnes, I Love You as Big as the World

for our daughter, Vidya

Table of Contents

foreword

Vidya's Tree opens with the phrase "When I was young" and closes with "*We're in Heaven—it's this beautiful garden.*"

Claire could not have intended the resonance with the context in which this chapbook appears. Her illness and death came quickly and unexpectedly, in the prime of her working life. Healthy and in her mid-forties, she was balancing a heavy teaching load, the raising of a young daughter, and the writing of her third book-length manuscript, not a chapbook of final poems.

As her grieving friend, I now isolate those phrases for my own purposes. I selfishly read "When I was young" as that two-year period in our early twenties when Claire and I were MFA candidates in creative writing at the University of Virginia, and take "Heaven" to be the "beautiful garden" in which Claire might now be enjoying a Satsuma orange tree with her parents. In context, of course, these are not what the phrases describe. "When I was young" refers to the poet's childhood, and "*We're in Heaven—it's this beautiful garden*" imagines the poet's deceased parents trying to speak to their living daughter. But the pleasure of poetry is that lines can do double duty, serving both the reader's and writer's purposes, and I'm sure Jon Loomis and Rajesh Ramakrishnan placed these bookends with this doubleness in mind.

I see those two years at UVA as the youth of Claire's career. She had just graduated from college and was able to make poetry the center of her life for the first time. She and I spent lengthy days and nights talking about poetry and our hopes for the future. We imagined who we might become as poets, where we might publish our first books, and how subject matter might come to mark us. Both American-born but having ongoing experiences shaped by race, we wondered to what extent we should write about Japan and China, countries more foreign than familiar, yet significant in ways we felt compelled to explore. What would become of us if we did or didn't address them? We conjectured about where we might end up living and how much writing time might be available in responsible adulthood. We also did our best to seize the present, often through the shared pleasures of cooking and eating, but our young ages and student status forced us to be future-oriented.

A quarter-century later, entrenched in responsible adulthood, I write after a different two years, two years of awareness that Claire is gone from the planet. Since the shock of her death, my daily life has not been much different on the surface—we lived many miles apart and had not been in regular touch over the years—but Claire was and is a lasting part of my creative foundation. Over the decades, sitting down to write or read, I felt assured by the knowledge that she was depicting the landscapes of her native L.A., asking tough questions about family, and imaginatively inhabiting the visual art she loved. I could hear her, in my head, setting me straight when I started second-guessing my drafts. Now I imagine her doing so from that "beautiful garden."

That is, I am forced to look backward where, with Claire, I used to look forward. Reading *Vidya's Tree*, I see the maturation of her longtime fascination with Frida Kahlo; the resolution of those early struggles with subject matter in "After the Earthquake and Tsunami, 2011"; her knowledge of meter and rhyme fully integrated into her deployment of free verse; and her gift for plain statement brought to an apex in "The Backyard Garden in Houston," constructed entirely of end-stopped lines, each its own sentence. These poems, like all good poems, are gifts to the future. The tragedy is that the future came so soon. I hope this collection will be gratefully received not only by Claire's existing readers but also by many who are hearing her voice for the first time, as well as by others who will hear it in another era, perhaps after all of us are gone.

—ADRIENNE SU

foreword

I first met Claire in the MFA program at the University of Virginia, back in 1991. It's not an overstatement to say that I felt, when I first arrived in a UVA classroom, as though I'd come from another planet—I was older, married, had been out of undergrad school for ten years, and couldn't have identified a sestina my first couple of weeks there if you'd tattooed it on my forehead. I was from small-town southeast Ohio—the Appalachian foothills—rough around the edges and given to unfiltered speech, and I was more than a little bit intimidated those first few weeks by the young, smart, talented poets in my cohort— mostly from the east coast, all from fancier schools than the Public Party U. I'd gone to, all capable of talking intelligently about famous contemporary poets I'd never heard of. I was writing poems about Bigfoot and Elvis and alien lizards and noir private eyes, very different (and much less stylish) than the poems the rest of the workshop was turning in. I was a big, easy target for my snarkier classmates, too, and it goes without saying, also, that I struggled—not sure what I was doing there, pretty sure I didn't belong—a goat among thoroughbreds.

But there was kindness in that workshop, too. Claire and Adrienne and a few others found things to like in those weird poems of mine, and seemed to take an interest in who I was and where I'd come from. That's what I remember most about Claire—what I adored—her kindness, her great compassion. But also, and this struck me right away, the depth of her talent. Even those early poems were striking— somehow they went straight to beauty, every time. Beauty! A rare and wonderful thing in this world. Honestly, it seemed like magic, and it was everywhere in her work.

Those, it seems to me, were Claire's considerable gifts—compassion and beauty. A poet could go a long way—could do anything, really—with those arrows in her quiver. These late poems of Claire's strike me the same way—more finished, perhaps, the surfaces a bit more polished as you might expect, the subjects more serious, the thinking deeper and more complex—but always she directs your eye to the beautiful thing, and everywhere you feel her beating heart, her love for the world, her family. This is the gift of these last poems, for me—there's something of Claire in every one, her energy, her mature being—like a bell that's been struck, that's still ringing.

I was honored when Raj, Claire's beloved husband, asked me to edit this collection. The poems here are drawn from a larger manuscript, also entitled *Vidya's Tree*, that ranged over the last decade or so of Claire's life. My hope was to select not just the strongest poems, because I felt they were all strong, but those that dealt with the subjects that seemed most pressing to her in the last few years of her life: her family, her husband, the art that fueled her imagination, her young daughter. What a pleasure it was to sit with Claire's late work for the month or so it took to order and assemble this chapbook! And how profoundly sad at times, and how joyous at others, when it seemed as though Claire were almost there with me, her voice in the room. And always the thought that these shouldn't be the last poems. That we ought, in a just world, to have years and years more of Claire and her work, this wealth of beauty and compassion, that bell, still ringing.

—JON LOOMIS

Vidya's Tree

ヴィディヤの木

विद्या का पेड़

Deep-Sea Magic

When I was young,
my grandfather
treasured me like a peach.

He struck the match
and lit the Eastern sun, netted
the carp swimming
over the wooden shingles
of our house.

The West L.A. sky
shrank between his knuckles.
The deep-sea, our swimming
pool, snagged our carved line
of detergent bottle tunas.

·

Today it is my husband
who loves me as my grandfather did,
and cherishes our daughter.

The Journey

For my Father, 1935-2011

Did dust vaporize, clouds' gravity collapse?
Did the sun's magnetosphere emit solar wind?

Did magnetic fields stop erosion
of the moon's surface, iced craters, lava?

Did the moon persist without any fields?
Did the earth's and moon's gravitational pull

raise the earth's tide currents to high water?
Did the sun's light spread to the Southern region?

Did planetesimals collide like a kiss,
followed by cratered debris and highlands?

Did you float and see other universes? Did you
stop and meet ancestors burst into song?

When My Daughter Wakes, I Tell Her

Your *Ta Ta*—grandfather, returned to Kerala
where two river banks meet. His spirit will wander

for thirteen days. *How much does she understand at 9 months?*

Each night, an eternity, she listens to her father's voice play back on the tape
  (she will destroy at 17 months when she realizes he's not there).
I pile pillows on the bed—a wall or cocoon, for her, playing,

  Deewana mujh sa nahin is ambar ke neeche—

One day she will ask what the lyrics mean.
  Will I tell her, *There is none as passionate as me under this sky—*

I'll probably say, "Ask your father."

Zagreb

February 2001

Tell me about the Fall's mildewed intrusions,
> how you get rid of them, how your writing flows from
you now. Tell me about your trip to the embassy,
> the Hungarian embassy, how the film glazing

your right eye clouds tonight's menu. Tell me how

> peace is limited to one island, *Hvar*, the island with
roads dating back to the Austro-Hungarian Empire,
> roads that haven't been widened or rebuilt, just paved.
Tell me how Hvar's roads narrow on the edge of a cliff,

> how the world's lavender comes from Hvar, the world's

marble from *Brac*. Tell me how you picked lavender,
> brought me lavender from Hvar, a shroud of Glad Wrap,
in B's pink bag with stars. I'll tell you I keep them in
> a clear jam jar, still see you planting lavender in your yard

for Croatia, splayed rays before the sun finally sets,

> as you nudge beets and Aggie carrots for dinner. I keep
the memory of that day alive, A. putting on make-up, her
> green eyes, a deep green like Chinese jade, *Good Fortune*
jade. I keep your words too, of telling me the sphere

you feel close to your father; it's not just a physical place,

but a psychological space. And Ivan's marble—marble
        from Brac, the same marble used in D.C., the White House.
Tell me how Croatian poppies are more sacred to you than
        lavender. They sprawl over the region your family is from.

After the Earthquake and Tsunami, 2011

1.   The Tree and Japanese Mother

Where piles of debris were tangled

in seaweed, she found
   a case of calligraphy brushes,

green tea Kit Kat Wrapper, crumpled
   school bag with cracked bento box—indicators

the class of children—her own son
   and daughter—had not survived.

•

What remained—a Gingko tree—
   fan shaped leaves

that withstood the bombings
   of Hiroshima and Nagasaki.

2.   *What the Parents of Sendai Did*

Their children slept on cardboard and lead mats.
They slept on nothing.

Their children ate rice crackers and juice.
They ate nothing.

Their children cried.
They never cried.

Their children worried.
They worried and swallowed iodine tablets.

They told their children,
Everything will be all right.

They told themselves,
Shikata ga nai—It cannot be helped.

They told themselves,
They would plant new trees and a garden—

3.   *Thirty Children At Kama Elementary School*

Despite the lack of plumbing
   the third floor became

their home. Each day
   the children sat at their desks

and waited. No one spoke
   to them. No one told them

their parents weren't coming.

4.   *Fukushima Girl in the Hospital*

There was no talk of radiation—
isotopes exceeding 30,

    nodules or cysts, or
    thyroid cancer. The Japanese way—

to resist telling the patient
she was dying, especially

    since she was a child.
    She knew what

the doctors and her parents
wouldn't admit—

    she'd never see marigolds
    at Disneyland, or bite into

an American hamburger—
She wouldn't be cremated

    (since the person who
    did them was dead).

She had loose hair
in a comic book,

a white tongue, jaundice. She kept
up with their charade—

"Don't worry—you'll get better."
She knew this was her last day,

and she wasn't afraid.

Bosch-Creature, After Seeing *The Garden of Earthly Delights*

I glimpse you titanium-blue,
eyes beneath
a moonish saucer:
floor upon
which a robed figure blows
a coral bagpipe,

and demons
prance their circuitous dance
over your face, birdish

and melancholy.
Let the stars
you forgot to paint

highlight the bartender
emptying the keg
in your eggshell stomach.

Let your legs
be twisted trunks,
and your ankles

rooted inside two green
boats, let them suggest your
Netherlanderish shoes.

After Eyeing a Paintwork of *Three Hands*

I see their blue, your blue hands overlapping, cheerful shade
of blue, unlike Picasso's blue in his blue period,

your blue filling blue longings for the surreal. If only
your blue hands could talk, the fingers could walk away with me,

play music, warn me when I step outside without my gloves,
the cold chilling the inside of my wrists and finger joints.

Your blue fingers could gesticulate signs and words to me
if fingers could dance and sweep me off...

What would I say to your blue fingers, set of three fingers?
The depths of your sonata ease me like three people.

As if blue fingers could tango, intuit a scarred heart's
fear of dispassion, of drowned seeds before they have a chance

to burst into full bloom, the air fragrant with flowering
vanilla stems—capsular fruit, bean pods, climbing orchids

waiting for spring, for the vodka to ferment the bean pods
into pure vanilla extract for baking and ice-cream,

to feed your blue fingers, splayed and waiting for something sweet—
sweet cream, *jocolatte*, midnight's blue Spanish sonatas.

What Frida Says

Green *is*   *warm and good light.*

Reddish Purple *is*   *blood of prickly pear.*

Brown *is*   *the earth.*

Yellow *is*   *madness, part sun and joy.*

Cobalt Blue *is*   *electricity and love.*

Leaf Green is   sadness and science.

Greenish Yellow *is*   *mystery—what phantoms wear.*

Dark Green *is*   *bad news and good business.*

Navy Blue *is*   *distance and tenderness.*

Magenta *is*   *bright blood and lips.*

Nothing is black.

Black, According to Frida

Nothing is black, nothing.
  Not the scars on my back, the cat, the freetail
bat, Granizo's fleas or Gertrude's centipede,
  or my brows, raven diving down.
Not the moon eclipsing the sun,
  not the air on the tip of this tack.

Not Judas, my paper mache Judas,
  hanging, dangling down. Not
the pictures of me squinting
  or is it reminiscing? The canopy
mirrors me, painting my plaits,
  my plaster corset. I still say,

Nothing is black. Not the cradle
  of clouds, or questions I ask out loud:
Will the death-god Pelona care? What will
  she say about my affairs?

Letter to Nick Muray

I am surrounded by
gypsy and tussock moths,
Mi niño, te adoro, mi Nick—

I blink red and it is you
in your black Essex,
your unbaked fingers
are on the wheel.
You steer left toward La Salle,
and say, *No*, to Blanche Heyes.

Mi niño, te adoro,
It is February 16, 1939.
I wear this Tehuana-red.
I brush life into a spider,
and sketch you, gold
inside a sweet-tart skull.

Can you hear him?
The parrot squawks,
No me pasa la cruda!
I'm so drunk I can't talk.

Nick, I have just slid down to sit.
Are you lying on the blue couch
with your white cape?
I'm tweezing Granizo's fleas.
I'm lighting a Savannah light—
Darling if you could see

the seed-size fleas
pepper themselves
across this page.
How is Joe Jinks?
Tell him,
my day stinks!

Letter to Diego

I am Diego's dust and Diego's wind,
his gangly and serpentine gladiola.
I, his gouache Señorita Frida,
weave Coyoacán thread, red.
My dear Diego, my dear—
June bugs cling to your
fat frog paunch.

It is six in the morning
and the turkeys are singing.
The swallows in the ocotillos
spread their twigs and chime,

Fridita, Niñita Chiquitita—

You're on the scaffold
in Detroit. Whose breasts
do you nudge into pillows?
My spine aches for a letter, Diego.
In San Angel, by the saguaro fence,
my fingerbones shake.
So I reach and light this marijuana

sucking the joint
like it is sugary cajeta. See Diego?
I climb my own death-bed scaffold.
Through the cleavage of clouds,
the baked vertebrae of your
celadon gallipott, I float
with Imogen, singing, Diego, my Diego,

the diadem, the walnut light,
stalagmite white strokes
of the vinca de mentas.
Diego, the peg leg
trunk of the apricot. Diego,
the turritella twist

of these pomegranate ribbons.
I knot them to Ignacio Aguirre—
You dream I am by the mistlethrush.
You dream my bitch-sister bravura.
Only I can turn your frog-eyes
sienna with sky-paint.

Lady Bartender Sitting Spineless for Diane Arbus

Night I work at Sergio's,
she says, "Give me a whiskey sour,
some onyx brows, lashes wispy
as tarantula hairs—"
So when she repeats, "Are you
free to photograph?"
I say, Sure.

Past Raji's, penguins dangle
from the awnings of Zulu.
Fairfax moon, stars that have
never glittered, powdery
as amphetamines.
Inside Diane's black
and white parlor, a Puerto Rican
lady waits. Diane snaps her
on the bed, and then me
lounging in this cemetery-pink
chair, still sticky in polyester
work clothes.

Diane points. "See that chenille
poodle? You have the same
bouffant hair—" I ignore her,
don't look.
So she hands me

size six boots and clothes,
saying, "Here, put this
leopard skin vest
over the turtleneck."

I button the skin
like a too tight bra.
Diane flashes her camera,
shoots close-ups of spit
frothing my lips.
"Shirle," she says.
"Sit spineless—"
I say, It's Angel or Katarina.

The stylus scrapes
it's four o'clock. I stretch,
tracing my thumb
to the wiry contours
of the jack of clubs
nailed to the wall behind me.
Diane asks, "You want
Schubert or the Blues?"
I answer, No.
I'm sick of the pianissimo.

My Husband Returns to America

with a suitcase, filled with chillis and vermicelli,
   silver anklets with miniature chimes

   to encourage our daughter to walk.

         •

When I show him the poem about colors
   he exclaims, "Chutney is reddish brown,

microbes are never cobalt blue,
   they're crystal violet."

About another poem, he says he remembers
   the movie the lyrics came from.

What I don't say—*I've made green chutney*
   from mint and cilantro—

The imagination has no limits.

Quill

A fishtail protrudes from
  the mouth of his doghead hat.
The blue figure dressed as
  an armored knight
sprints toward the naked men
  clustered below the tree.
Or is the knight's face violet,
  riding the cloaked, eelheaded beast?
The eel might be salamander
  or iguana, the way the brass
studded harness clamps
  its turquoise mouth shut.
The arm from nowhere grips
  a needled ax, its elbow
juts out like a Malibu pigeon,
  with one tangible wing,
cinnabar stroke to the right.

The Backyard Garden in Houston

Grass seeds and shifting salamanders wake the creatures below.
Beetles trundle through the top layer of fertile soil.

Crisp divots of transplanting absorb air and light.
Dispersal of ladybugs inhibits the spread of aphids.

How clever the chameleon is to camouflage itself as clover.
And the gopher, idiosyncratic as ever, lapses from furrowing.

Irritated by the musty commotion, it gnaws the inveterate pipes.
The soaker hose responds with trickles, then a surge of warm water.

It's the chlorinated kind that strips hair of its natural shade.
In this city, hard water bleaches every head with locks.

My hair, once black, turns red, dulls from rust to brown.
In mirrors under halogen, I see haphazard strands of orange.

Chlorinating kills the germinating suspects.
Fluoridating keeps the tooth enamel from wearing.

A fledgling lands on the lip of a brimming seed jar.
The seeds spill, frightening the fledgling into awkward flight.

The wind tosses blue buttons, phlox, and sunflower seeds.
The ground needs something besides Harlequin beetles.

In the end everything thrives to wither and reseed itself.
Scientists say creatures will plant, continue to thrive.

The raven, eyeing carrion, drops a half-eaten apricot.

The Distraction

Houston, Texas

When our daughter smiles and cries,
   my husband carries her outside
and sings songs in Hindi,
   crooning, *Don't worry,*
It's just Vishnu hiding behind a Lotus Leaf. To distract her,
   he points out the Spinach and Holy Basil,
the Satsuma and avocado tree,
   Elephant Ears flapping
above the dirt and concrete, fire ants
   climbing from cracks. Our cat, *Happy Joe*, sits
on the window ledge peering out at us.

When she says, *Bo-Bo,* her word for cat,
my husband whispers, *Vishnu's back!*
   It's then I see my father in her face,
her *Ta Ta—grandfather* in her feet,
   just as I'd seen my mother in my niece.

   O my Daughter, you remind me
our parents are still with us—

Vidya's Tree

In Urdu, Gulzar means "garden in bloom."

.

Gulzar, a poet who made language *bloom*, wrote the following lyrics to a song in a Hindi movie. A translation of the Hindi words into English sounds something like this: "A paper boat does not have a destination as a traveler. Any bank that meets another bank is the traveler's destination."

.

Remember *this* translation came from your father.

.

He has since forgotten the movie the lyrics came from.

.

Poignant, subtle, the image Gulzar described is in one sense a Romantic illusion because banks will never meet. With banks always parallel to each other, the person continues traveling. When he or she is asked, "Where are you traveling? What's your destination?" he or she will answer, "My destination is a place where two river banks meet."

.

Anniket means "he who travels—is at home everywhere."

.

Vidya— "Righteous Knowledge."

.

Just as wings to a bird will enable it to fly—even soar—the wind is like wings because the effect is the same. The wind aids in the bird's flight from point to point. In America, a kite is made of paper, cloth, wood, and string. In India, a kite circles its prey, dives in—*to kill*, spread with talons, beak, and feathers.

.

Your ancestors—descendants of the samurai, Brahmins, Vishnu, mythologized Japanese crane—relied on salt-air to withstand the turbulence of flight. In actuality, their flight was a figure of speech since most arrived by ship.

.

Vidya, your *TaTa*—grandfather— returned to Kerala's river banks.

.

In Thrissur, your father cradles *TaTa*, offers red petals to Hindu
goddesses.

•

In America you turn—dream in syllables—I give you my life,
and *TaTa*'s last words—*Smile Baby Vidya, always smile* . . .

For My Daughter

Don't cry Little One,
it's only Vishnu
hiding the branch.
Don't cry,
He'll bring it back.
For now, smile
at the lizard worshipping
the sun.

When you miss the warmth
of my womb. I miss
your kicks and flutters inside,
how you would dance
when we ate vanilla
ice-cream and yogurt,
kiwi popsicle. I will soothe you in my arms But now
I get to cradle you
in my arms, as you blink
back and smile at me.

Your father held you first
under the light
after you were born.
Now he holds and sings
you songs in Hindi, pointing
out the spinach and Holy Basil,
the small orange and avocado tree,
the Elephant's Ears leaves

flapping above the dirt
and concrete, fire ants
climbing from the cracks.
One day you will inherit
this house. When we are gone,
don't cry. Like Vishnu,
we are always with you.

You are the gift from above,
miracle of my life.

House in Tucson, Arizona

My parents will never see the Satsuma orange tree
or daughter I gave birth to in October.

In the hills, where they once lived,
lavender and evening primrose are in full bloom.

The stench of javelinas permeates the air.
Lizards lounge, waiting for my parents to swat flies.

How does one tell reptiles their best friends are gone?

Water trickles in miniature rivulets, from
the Jacuzzi to the pool. The sound is

calm, bright—as my parents' existence.
Their house, once dark, filled with this light—

their souls or spirits singing to let go,
celebrate, as if they're saying,

We're in Heaven—it's this beautiful garden.

Afterword: A Tribute for Claire Kageyama-Ramakrishnan as a Letter to Her Daughter Vidya

Charlottesville, Virginia, May 21, 2016

Dear Vidya,

It is difficult to describe Claire to you, because I knew her when she was a young woman, before you and your father entered the picture—and it's always hard to imagine one's mother or father as anything other than one's parents. But I will try.

I met Claire in the late summer of 1991, at the University of Virginia Creative Writing Program's annual welcome picnic. She was one of five new graduate poets, and my first impression was of a soft-spoken but strong personality. What I also remember about that afternoon of barbecue and wiffle ball and badminton by a county lake was your mother's intensity—it was as if, balled up inside this tiny dynamo, was a vortex of lightning. Not that she was repressed or holding anything back; in fact, she was using her intensity to power her passion. And her passion was poetry—she was determined to hone her craft, to stretch her voice, to learn how to contain multitudes using the sparest, simplest language possible. She was fearless, both in and out of the classroom, on and off the page—and as such, she refused to draw a line between her life as an artist and her experiences as a citizen of the world. She was impatient and a perfectionist, which could have been a volatile combination were it not for Claire's sense of humor, which was wicked, ironic, and utterly delightful. That Claire was one of the few students my husband and I trusted to babysit our daughter from the age of eight to ten says it all—she was that good, that witty, that caring.

I keep coming back to one of her marvelous poems, "Origins of an Impulse", because in it I can hear the young Claire's quiet, insistent voice as she argued a point or expressed incredulity over a so-called human interest story on the news. It is the voice of a woman who somehow knew—even then in my Advanced Poetry Writing Seminar, back when the future hadn't happened yet—that she was speaking to you, her daughter, when she wrote:

> It happened
> when I saw my mother's face in my face,
> when I saw her face in my niece's face.
> It happened with love, the impulse to write.

Dearest Vidya, a time will come when you will have grown old enough to read and understand the poetry your mother has left you. Cherish this beautiful legacy; it is a rare and extraordinary gift which will suffuse your memories and help keep her close to your heart.

With my greatest affection,
Rita Dove

About the Author

Claire Kageyama-Ramakrishnan was born in Santa Monica, California, and raised in Los Angeles. Claire was a mother, a wife, a sister, a friend, a neighbor, an accomplished poet, scholar, teacher, and animal-lover. She received her B.A. in English from Loyola Marymount University in L.A. She went on to earn an M.F.A. in Creative Writing (Poetry) from the University of Virginia, where she was a Henry Hoyns Fellow (under the mentorship of Rita Dove); an M.A. in Literature from the University of California, Berkeley; and a Ph.D. in Literature and Creative Writing from the University of Houston, where she was a Cambor Fellow. She published two acclaimed books of poetry: *Shadow Mountain* (Four Way Books, 2008) and *Bear, Diamonds and Crane* (Four Way Books, 2011). *Shadow Mountain* was the 2006 winner of the Four Way Books Intro Prize in Poetry.

Claire Kageyama-Ramakrishnan, Ph.D., passed away in 2016 and is survived by her husband, Raj, and their daughter, Vidya.